I SPY
THANKSGIVING

Copyright © 2020 by The Pretty Awesome Gift Company

All rights reserved. This book or any portion thereof
may not be reproduced or used in any manner whatsoever
without the express written permission of the publisher
except for the use of brief quotations in a book review.
First Printing, 2020

I SPY WITH MY LITTLE EYE SOMETHING BEGINNING WITH...

A IS FOR ACORN

Now practice tracing the letter A

I SPY WITH MY LITTLE EYE 3 FLOWERS

I SPY WITH MY LITTLE EYE SOMETHING BEGINNING WITH...

B IS FOR BREAD

Now practice tracing the letter B

I SPY WITH MY LITTLE EYE SOMETHING THAT GOES HOOT!

AN OWL GOES HOOT!

I SPY WITH MY LITTLE EYE SOMETHING BEGINNING WITH...

C IS FOR CORN

Now practice tracing the letter C

I SPY WITH MY LITTLE EYE
3 LEAVES

THERE THEY ARE! DID YOU SPOT THEM?

I SPY WITH MY LITTLE EYE SOMETHING BEGINNING WITH...

D IS FOR DUCK

Now practice tracing the letter D

I SPY WITH MY LITTLE EYE 5 MUGS

I SPY WITH MY LITTLE EYE SOMETHING BEGINNING WITH...

E IS FOR EGG

Now practice tracing the letter E

A MOUSE GOES SQUEAK!

I SPY WITH MY LITTLE EYE SOMETHING BEGINNING WITH...

F IS FOR FISH

Now practice tracing the letter F

I SPY WITH MY LITTLE EYE
2 SQUIRRELS

THERE THEY ARE!
DID YOU SPOT THEM?

I SPY WITH MY LITTLE EYE SOMETHING BEGINNING WITH...

G IS FOR GOOSE

Now practice tracing the letter G

I SPY WITH MY LITTLE EYE SOMETHING BEGINNING WITH...

H

IS FOR HAM

Now practice tracing the letter H

I SPY WITH MY LITTLE EYE SOMETHING THAT GOES MOOOO!

A COW GOES MOOOO!

I SPY WITH MY LITTLE EYE SOMETHING BEGINNING WITH...

IS FOR
ICE CREAM

Now practice tracing the letter I

I SPY WITH MY LITTLE EYE
3 PUMPKINS

J

IS FOR JAM

Now practice tracing the letter J

I SPY WITH MY LITTLE EYE 3 OWLS

I SPY WITH MY LITTLE EYE SOMETHING BEGINNING WITH...

K IS FOR KITE

Now practice tracing the letter K

I SPY WITH MY LITTLE EYE SOMETHING THAT GOES MEOOW!

A CAT GOES MEOOW!

L IS FOR LEAF

Now practice tracing the letter L

I SPY WITH MY LITTLE EYE
6 ACORNS

THERE THEY ARE!
DID YOU SPOT THEM?

M IS FOR MOUSE

Now practice tracing the letter M

I SPY WITH MY LITTLE EYE 3 JUMPERS

THERE THEY ARE!!!
DID YOU SPOT THEM?

I SPY WITH MY LITTLE EYE SOMETHING BEGINNING WITH...

N IS FOR NUT

Now practice tracing the letter N

I SPY WITH MY LITTLE EYE SOMETHING BEGINNING WITH...

O IS FOR OVEN

Now practice tracing the letter O

I SPY WITH MY LITTLE EYE
3 TREES

I SPY WITH MY LITTLE EYE SOMETHING BEGINNING WITH...

P IS FOR PUMPKIN

Now practice tracing the letter P

P P P P P P P

P P P P P P P

I SPY WITH MY LITTLE EYE 7 APPLES

Q IS FOR QUINCE

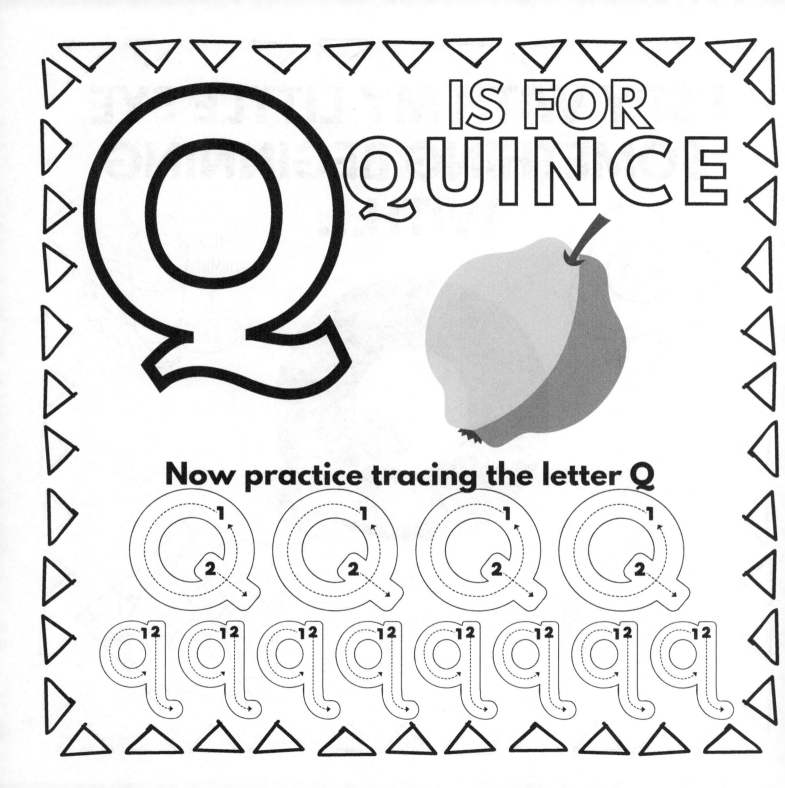

Now practice tracing the letter Q

I SPY WITH MY LITTLE EYE SOMETHING THAT GOES RAWR!

A LION GOES RAWR!

R IS FOR RAVEN

Now practice tracing the letter R

I SPY WITH MY LITTLE EYE
4 BALLOONS

THERE THEY ARE!
DID YOU SPOT THEM?

I SPY WITH MY LITTLE EYE SOMETHING BEGINNING WITH...

I SPY WITH MY LITTLE EYE 3 BUGS

THERE THEY ARE!!!
DID YOU SPOT THEM?

T IS FOR TURKEY

Now practice tracing the letter T

I SPY WITH MY LITTLE EYE SOMETHING THAT GOES QUACK!

I SPY WITH MY LITTLE EYE SOMETHING BEGINNING WITH...

U IS FOR UMBRELLA

Now practice tracing the letter U

I SPY WITH MY LITTLE EYE
6 MUSHROOMS

I SPY WITH MY LITTLE EYE SOMETHING BEGINNING WITH...

V IS FOR VEGETABLES

Now practice tracing the letter V

I SPY WITH MY LITTLE EYE 7 COBWEBS

THERE THEY ARE! DID YOU SPOT THEM ALL?

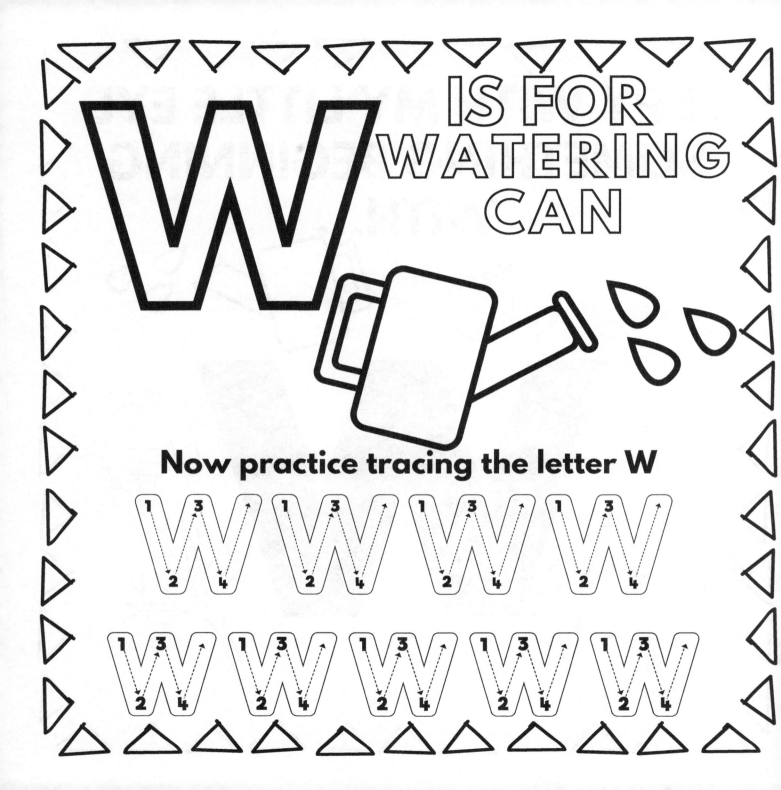

W IS FOR WATERING CAN

Now practice tracing the letter W

I SPY WITH MY LITTLE EYE SOMETHING BEGINNING WITH...

X IS FOR XYLOPHONE

Now practice tracing the letter X

I SPY WITH MY LITTLE EYE SOMETHING BEGINNING WITH...

Y IS FOR YAM

Now practice tracing the letter Y

I SPY WITH MY LITTLE EYE SOMETHING BEGINNING WITH...

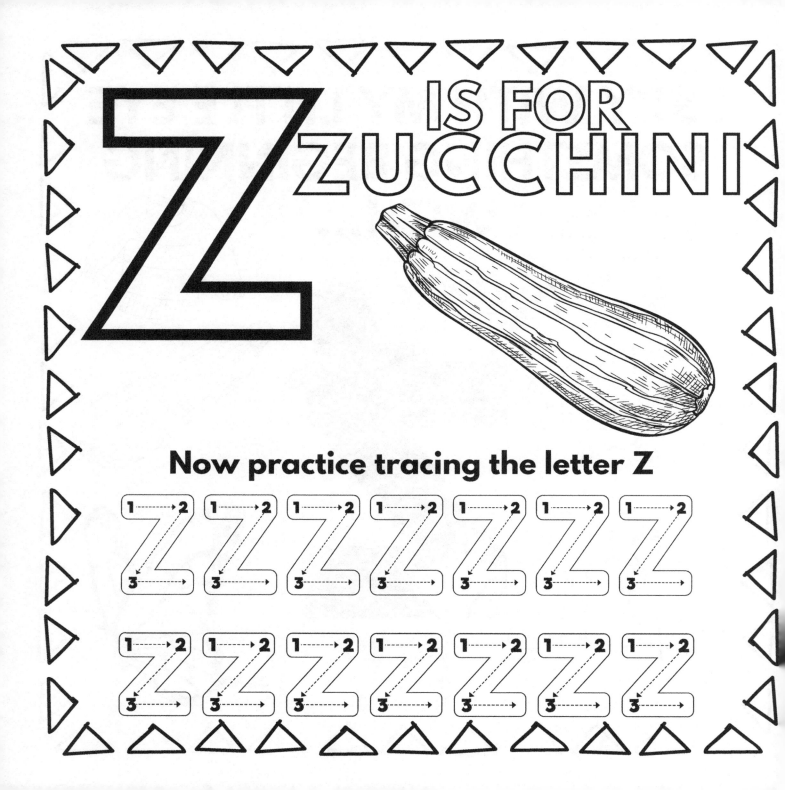

Z IS FOR ZUCCHINI

Now practice tracing the letter Z

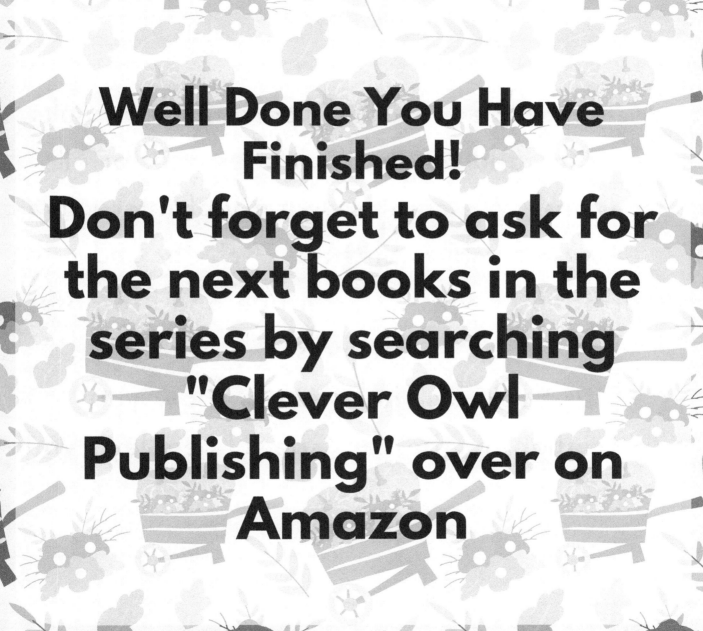

Well Done You Have Finished!
Don't forget to ask for the next books in the series by searching "Clever Owl Publishing" over on Amazon

We specialize in creating personalized books for kids and adults of all ages and for all occasions. We create a variety of interactive books such as Birthday Activity and Affirmation books to Gratitude and Prompted Journals.

Our books will help you to show your appreciation for the very special people in your life.

Made in the USA
Monee, IL
11 August 2022

11442463R00057